Noah and the Rainbow

An Ancient Story
Retold by Max Bolliger

Translated by Clyde Robert Bulla

With Pictures by Helga Aichinger

THOMAS Y. CROWELL COMPANY   New York

L.C. Card 72-76361   ISBN 0-690-58448-2   0-690-58449-0 (LB)

Designed by Barbara Kohn Isaac

Noah and
the Rainbow

NOAH was a good man.
He was six hundred years old.
One night God called to Noah
and said:
"Build an ark, a great boat of wood,
three hundred cubits long,
fifty cubits wide,
and thirty cubits high.
Build it with three floors—
one above the other.
Build it with a window at the top
and a door on the side,
and coat it with tar
inside and out."

Noah did as God had told him.
He built an ark,
and his three sons,
Shem, Ham, and Japheth,
helped him.

When they had finished,
they took plenty of food and clothing
into the ark.
They made room
for the animals —
the wild and the tame,
the small and the large,
the strong and the weak,
the slow and the fast —
a pair of every kind.
For this also was God's command to Noah.

As every animal
found his place,
Noah, too, went into the ark,
and his family with him —
his wife,
his sons,
and their wives
and children.

The other people laughed
at what Noah had done.
"What is the use of a boat on dry land?" they asked.
Their scorn did not trouble Noah.
But God was angry with them
because they did not fear Him,
and because they laughed.

When Noah, with plenty of food and clothing,
was settled in the ark
with his family —
his wife,
his sons,
and their wives
and children —
God sent a great rain
to fall upon the earth.

Forty days and forty nights
it rained.

The brooks turned to rivers,
the lakes became oceans.
It rained and rained and rained.
All the waters rose
and spread across the earth.

The people fled to the hills.
They fled to the mountains.
But the water rose and rose.
It covered the hills,
it covered the mountains,
and every living thing on the earth
had to die.

But Noah's wooden ark
was carried high and safe
on the water.
The children
looked from the window
and saw
the hills disappear
and the mountains disappear.
Then,
for one hundred and fifty days,
they saw
from the window
only water and sky.

But God had not forgotten
Noah
and his family in the ark.
He had not forgotten
the animals in the ark.
After one hundred and fifty days
He let the wind blow
the clouds apart,
and the rain stopped.
He let the sun shine,
and the water slowly
began to sink.

The mountain peaks
appeared again,
and one day
the ark came to rest
on the flat top of a mountain
called Ararat.

The children wanted to climb out,
but Noah made them wait.
Only after forty days
did he open the window
and let a raven fly out.
The raven saw nothing but water
and, deep in the water, a single seashell.
The bird fluttered here and there,
sat for a moment on Noah's hand,
then flew back into the ark.

After seven days
Noah opened the window again
and let a dove fly out.
The dove soon returned,
sat for a moment on Noah's hand,
then flew back into the ark.
After another seven days
Noah let the dove fly out a second time.
She did not return until evening,
when she sat on Noah's hand,
then flew back into the ark.

But in her beak
she brought an olive twig.
Now Noah knew that trees
were beginning to grow again
on the earth.

He waited seven more days,
then he let the dove fly out
for the third time.
She did not return again.
Now Noah,
with his family
and all the animals,
left the ark.

Once more the earth was dry,
and the mountains,
the hills, and the valleys.
The brooks ran in their beds,
and the lakes moved in their basins.

Noah and his family were glad
to feel the earth
under their feet again,
and Noah thanked God.

But the fields and plains
were bare.
All that man had planted
was washed away.
Nothing that man had built was left
except the ark.

God heard Noah's prayer of thanks.
He looked at the ruined earth
and had pity
on Noah, whom He loved,
and on his family —
his wife,
his three sons,
their wives
and children,
and all the children of these children,
who were not yet born.

He stretched a rainbow across the sky
and said to Noah:
"You are a good man
and have obeyed me faithfully.
Now I make you this promise.
Never again will a flood
destroy the earth.
From now on there will be sowing and harvest,
cold and heat,
day and night
forever.
The rainbow will always remind people
of this promise."

At that, Noah rejoiced,
and so did his family —
his wife,
his three sons,
and their wives
and all the children.